50 DAYS OF
PRAYING GOD'S PROMISES

VOLUME ONE

CJ and Shelley Hitz

50 Days of Praying God's Promises
By CJ and Shelley Hitz

Published by Body and Soul Publishing LLC
Colorado Springs, CO 80904
© 2021 CJ and Hitz

ISBN: 978-1-946118-18-9

Unless otherwise indicated, all Scripture quotations are taken from the Holy Bible, The World English Bible (WEB), public domain.

Contents

Living Your Faith

Remain In Me

Grateful, Thankful, Blessed

God With Us

New Beginnings

Designed By God

Set Free

Conclusion

Introduction

There's something powerful when our prayers are rooted in God's Word. The Scriptures provide rich soil that our prayers can continually draw upon in order to grow and thrive.

Hebrews 4:12 says, "For the word of God is *living and active*, and sharper than any two-edged sword, piercing even to the dividing of soul and spirit, of both joints and marrow, and is able to discern the thoughts and intentions of the heart." (Emphasis mine)

Living and Active.

That would be the opposite of dead and inactive which has sometimes described how our prayer lives have felt.

Have you ever found your prayer times to be stale and lifeless? Perhaps you take time to pray only to lose focus while finding yourself at a sudden loss for words?

Praying according to God's Word can add focus while also reminding us of God's timeless promises. It can be the kindling that the Holy Spirit uses to light a fire of deep and meaningful prayer time with our Father.

And a little can go a long way. One verse of scripture can provide the base that helps launch a prayer from our heart for the next several minutes. Whether we're reading the words of David crying out to God in the Psalms, Paul's encouraging words to the Church, or the comforting and convicting words of Jesus, the same Spirit that guided them will also guide us as we draw upon these words of Truth.

Our hope is that these fifty days of praying God's promises will help spark a habit in your own life of praying with God's Word in mind. We encourage you to read the daily scripture multiple times to allow it to sink deep into your mind, heart, and spirit. After reading the prayer for that day, feel free to write out your own prayer in the space below or in your own journal.

Rather than rushing through the book in one sitting, we hope you'll meditate and savor one day at a time in order to allow God to transform your heart and mind one promise at a time.

May you experience a freshness and vibrancy in your prayer time as you plant yourself in the life-giving soil of God's Promises found in the Bible!

CJ & Shelley

Let
Hope
Rise

Day One

SCRIPTURE:

"This hope we have as an anchor of the soul, a hope both sure and steadfast and entering into that which is within the veil." - Hebrews 6:19

PRAYER:

Jesus, thank you for being the anchor for our souls. No matter how strong the storms in our lives become, we trust You as the anchor that holds. You are trustworthy, Lord, and we place our hope in You alone. Your sacrifice provided direct access to Your Father. Our only response is to fall to our knees and worship. It's in Your wonderful name we pray, Amen.

Day Two

SCRIPTURE:

"Now may the God of hope fill you with all joy and peace in believing, that you may abound in hope, in the power of the Holy Spirit." - Romans 15:13

PRAYER:

Father, we acknowledge You as our Source of hope. Thank you for the promise that we can be completely filled with joy and peace as a result of trusting in You. Thank you Holy Spirit for giving us an overflow of confident hope. We place no confidence in the emptiness of our flesh or the false peace of the world. You are our Source and everything else is simply a resource. We run into the halls of heaven to draw close to You Abba (Daddy). It's in Jesus' name we pray, Amen.

Day Three

SCRIPTURE:

"For I know the thoughts that I think toward you," says the LORD, "thoughts of peace, and not of evil, to give you hope and a future." - Jeremiah 29:11

PRAYER:

Father, we trust the plans You have for us. We know You are good in everything you do. Even when we're going through rough waters, we know it's part of Your great plan. Even when we don't always see or feel You, we trust that You are right beside us. Thank you for the promise that You are working ALL things together for the good of those who love You. Nothing is wasted in Your Kingdom. You are the God who holds our future and we place our full hope in You alone. In Jesus' mighty name we pray, Amen.

Day Four

SCRIPTURE:

"Be strong, and let your heart take courage, all you who hope in the Lord." - Psalm 31:24

PRAYER:

Father, we place our hope in You, Jesus, and the Holy Spirit. There is no life apart from You. We are weak and fragile in our own strength. You are our strength and courage for anything we face. Replace our fear with Your faith. We trade in our panic for Your peace. We ask You to calm our chaos. In Your presence, demons flee. You are worthy of every ounce of praise and worship Your creation can muster. Fill us Holy Spirit that we might walk with courage and boldness everywhere we go. It's in Jesus' name we pray, Amen.

You
are
Safe

Day Five

SCRIPTURE:

"The fear of man proves to be a snare, but whoever puts his trust in the Lord is kept safe."
- Proverb 29:25

PRAYER:

Father, we place our trust in You alone. Apart from You, we walk on fragile ground that can give way at any moment. We ask that You drive away all fear of man and unproductive thoughts in our lives. Thank you for preserving us despite the poor decisions we may have made in the past. In Jesus' name, Amen.

Day Six

SCRIPTURE:

"He will cover you with his feathers. Under his wings you will take refuge. His faithfulness is your shield and rampart." - Psalm 91:4

PRAYER:

Father, we seek refuge under your loving care. We make our home in You as storms come our way. Thank you for the protection we experience as we stand behind Your faithful promises day and night. We take comfort in knowing You are always faithful even when we are unfaithful. In Jesus' name we pray, Amen.

Day Seven

SCRIPTURE:

"I have set the Lord always before me. Because he is at my right hand, I shall not be moved." - Psalm 16:8

PRAYER:

Father, we take courage knowing You are always walking beside us. No matter what obstacles we face, we are victorious because of the death and resurrection of Your Son. When spiritual bullies approach us, they run the other direction after seeing You next to us. We walk in confidence knowing we're on the winning team! In Jesus' mighty name we pray, Amen.

Day Eight

SCRIPTURE:

"The Lord's name is a strong tower: the righteous run to him, and are safe." - Proverb 18:10

PRAYER:

Father, You are our place of safety and rest. Like an impenetrable fortress, You provide refuge for those who choose to run to You. No matter where we find ourselves, no border can prevent us from running to You. Not only do You provide safe shelter in the midst of storms, You also calm those storms with a simple command. There is no other name outside of Your Son where safety can be found. It's in the powerful name of Jesus we pray, Amen.

There is
is
More

Day Nine

SCRIPTURE:

"But God, being rich in mercy, for his great love with which He loved us, even when we were dead through our trespasses, made us alive together with Christ—by grace you have been saved." - Ephesians 2:4-5

PRAYER:

Father, we thank you for the extravagant mercy and grace you have shown us in the gift of Your Son. Without Jesus, we would be dead. All of our human efforts are lifeless. We acknowledge our complete and utter poverty without the riches You alone offer us. Thank you for raising us from death to life. It's in the wonderful name of Jesus we pray, Amen.

Day Ten

SCRIPTURE:

"The Lord God says to these bones: 'Behold, I will cause breath to enter into you, and you will live.'"
- Ezekiel 37:5

PRAYER:

Father, we thank you for breathing new life into all the dry areas of our lives. Without that breath of life, we would be nothing but a pile of dry bones. You have transformed this lifeless clay into something that bears Your very image. Holy Spirit, fill us from head to toe with your life-giving power and help us to be people who speak life into those we encounter on this journey. We ask this in Jesus' name, Amen.

Day Eleven

SCRIPTURE:

"It is the Spirit who gives life. The flesh profits nothing. The words that I speak to you are spirit, and are life." - John 6:63

PRAYER:

Father, thank you for giving us an alternative to relying on our flesh. Jesus, thank you for voluntarily leaving Your place in Heaven in order to take on human flesh and dwell among us. Everywhere your feet walked saw the darkness flee in every direction. You embodied Life itself and gave us a delicious appetizer of what is to come for those who love You. Give us the words of spirit and life that we can then pass along to others. In Jesus' name we pray, Amen.

Day Twelve

SCRIPTURE:

"Because Christ also suffered for sins once, the righteous for the unrighteous, that he might bring you to God, being put to death in the flesh, but made alive in the Spirit." - 1 Peter 3:18

PRAYER:

Father, we fall on our faces before You in worship and adoration. We lift the name of Jesus up high for all He accomplished through suffering. Holy Spirit, we stand in awe of your life-giving power that brought us from a dead and lifeless existence. Oh the joy that wells up from within as we experience the weight of our sin falling off! May that joy infect and whet the appetites of those You place in our paths. In the matchless name of Jesus we pray, Amen.

Bridge to Life

Day Thirteen

SCRIPTURE:

"For all have sinned, and fall short of the glory of God." - Romans 3:23

PRAYER:

Father, I confess that I have sinned against you and fall woefully short of your glorious standard. Rather than make elaborate excuses, I humbly admit my guilt and ask that you have mercy on me, a sinner. It's in the wonderful name of Jesus I pray, Amen.

Day Fourteen

SCRIPTURE:

"For the wages of sin is death, but the free gift of God is eternal life in Christ Jesus our Lord." - Romans 6:23

PRAYER:

Father, even though I deserve an eternal death sentence, I'm overwhelmed with gratitude and worship for the eternal life I've been given through your Son, Jesus Christ. You have given me pure grace when I could offer You nothing but my life in return. I humbly receive Your free gift. In Jesus' name I pray, Amen.

Day Fifteen

SCRIPTURE:

"But God commends his own love toward us, in that while we were yet sinners, Christ died for us." - Romans 5:8

PRAYER:

Father, we fall to our knees in worship and reverence as a result of what Your Son accomplished on our behalf. Though we've sinned greatly, Jesus willingly shed His precious blood as full payment for our salvation. Help us to constantly remember this Gift of all gifts. In the powerful name of Jesus we pray, Amen.

Day Sixteen

SCRIPTURE:

"For by grace you have been saved through faith, and that not of yourselves; it is the gift of God, not of works, that no one would boast." - Ephesians 2:8-9

PRAYER:

Father, what a gift we have been given! None of us could ever boast in Your presence. None of us could ever bring anything of value as a means of payment. Fill us with a desire to bless others as a result of the blessing You have lavished upon us. Thank you for this extravagant grace You have shown us. In Jesus' name we pray, Amen.

Day Seventeen

SCRIPTURE:

"Behold, I stand at the door and knock. If anyone hears my voice and opens the door, then I will come in to him, and will dine with him, and he with me." - Revelation 3:20

PRAYER:

Jesus, we gladly open the door of our hearts to You. In fact, please enjoy access to every last room or closet in our house. We desire to submit every area of our lives to You. What a joy and privilege to enjoy Your fellowship and the community of Your people. Help us to always hear your knock on our door. It's in Your name we pray, Amen.

Day Eighteen

SCRIPTURE:

"Most certainly I tell you, he who hears my word, and believes him who sent me, has eternal life, and doesn't come into judgment, but has passed out of death into life." - John 5:24

PRAYER:

Father, we believe You sent Your Son into this world to save us from destruction. We acknowledge there is no other way to salvation outside of Jesus. When we were well on our way toward eternal death, You reached into our lives and brought us into Your glorious light. Give us ears to hear and eyes to see the wonder of Your Word. It's in the glorious name of Jesus we pray, Amen.

Living your Faith

Day Nineteen

SCRIPTURE:

"Therefore if anyone is in Christ, he is a new creation. The old things have passed away. Behold, all things have become new." - 2 Corinthians 5:17

PRAYER:

Father, we thank you for the new life we have in Christ and the freedom to leave our old life behind. You have done a miracle deep within me by giving me new desires, new dreams, and new priorities. The sin I used to love, I now hate. This glorious gospel I used to hate, I now love. What I used to see in black and white, I now see in color. You have put an extra hop in my step and I can't help but praise You with every breath! In Jesus' name I pray, Amen.

Day Twenty

SCRIPTURE:

"One who has my commandments and keeps them, that person is one who loves me. One who loves me will be loved by my Father, and I will love him, and will reveal myself to him." - John 14:21

PRAYER:

Father, we ask that you give us a deep desire to obey your Word in Christ. Deposit a supernatural love into our hearts that we can share with others. Fill us with your Holy Spirit in order to accomplish Your will on earth. Thank you for the love you have lavished on us by making us sons and daughters in Your family. It's in the wonderful name of Jesus we pray, Amen.

Day Twenty One

SCRIPTURE:

"Every Scripture is God-breathed and profitable for teaching, for reproof, for correction, and for instruction in righteousness." - 2 Timothy 3:16

PRAYER:

Father, what a gift You have given us in the Scriptures! Just as You breathed these glorious words into existence, so You have breathed new life into our dead souls. Increase our appetite for the Scriptures and nourish our souls with each living word. Open our eyes to the treasures found throughout these Scriptures. Keep us from deception as we receive Your correction in righteousness. In Jesus' name we pray, Amen.

Day Twenty Two

SCRIPTURE:

"If you remain in me, and my words remain in you, you will ask whatever you desire, and it will be done for you." - John 15:7

PRAYER:

Father, we ask you for an overwhelming desire to remain in your Son. May the words of Jesus always be on the tip of our tongue and ready to be shared with a hungry world. We desire to have hearts that long for You alone. We also ask that our lost friends and family be drawn out of the darkness and into Your glorious light. We ask these things in Jesus' name, Amen.

Day Twenty Three

SCRIPTURE:

"For where two or three are gathered together in my name, there I am in the middle of them." - Matthew 18:20

PRAYER:

Father, we thank you for the wonderful promise that where two or three of Your children are gathered, your Son is right in their midst. What a gift we have in Jesus! Thank you for the 'all-access pass' we have when we gather in the Name above all names. Our hearts are warmed in Your presence. In that mighty name of Jesus we pray, Amen.

Day Twenty Four

SCRIPTURE:

"For I am not ashamed of the Good News of Christ, because it is the power of God for salvation for everyone who believes, for the Jew first, and also for the Greek." - Romans 1:16

PRAYER:

Father, we ask that you remove every ounce of shame in our lives. Like your servant Paul, may we be unashamed to live out and proclaim the Good News of Christ. Give us a Spirit-led boldness to share this message of salvation with those we cross paths with. Lead us to people who are ripe to hear and believe the greatest message ever told. Thank you for the privilege we have to be Kingdom messengers. In Jesus' name we pray, Amen.

Remain in Me

Day Twenty Five

SCRIPTURE:

"Remain in Me, and I in you. As the branch can't bear fruit by itself, unless it remains in the vine, so neither can you, unless you remain in Me." - John 15:4

PRAYER:

Father, we confess our dryness and inability to produce any lasting fruit apart from your Son. Give us a deep desire to be completely dependent upon the nourishment only You, the Son, and the Spirit provide. Thank you for the privilege of being a branch attached to Jesus, our Tree of LIfe. In the wonderful name of Jesus we pray, Amen.

Day Twenty Six

SCRIPTURE:

"If you remain in Me, and My words remain in you, you will ask whatever you desire, and it will be done for you." - John 15:7

PRAYER:

Jesus, thank you for the promise that if we remain in You, we can ask for whatever we desire and it will be done. We confess that many of our desires aren't rooted in You. Give us eternal desires that originate in your heart. Break our hearts with the things that break yours. Fill us with Your words that come from heaven. Pull us back when we begin to stray from Your Presence. It's in Your mighty name we pray, Amen.

Day Twenty Seven

SCRIPTURE:

"If you keep My commandments, you will remain in My love; even as I have kept My Father's commandments, and remain in His love." - John 15:10

PRAYER:

Father, we acknowledge that we have broken Your commandments. We have not loved You, the Son, or the Spirit with all of our heart, soul, mind, and strength. We have not loved our neighbors as ourselves. And yet, here you are, still drawing us back to Your love and tenderness as a parent with a rebellious child. We know all Your commandments are summed up in a word: Love. Fill us with a supernatural love that could only originate with You. It's in Jesus' name we pray, Amen.

Day Twenty Eight

SCRIPTURE:

"By this we know that we remain in Him and He in us, because He has given us of His Spirit." - 1 John 4:13

PRAYER:

Father, thank you for the deposit of your Holy Spirit as proof that we are Yours. In those moments when we're tempted to wander from Your presence, we are gently prodded by the Spirit to reconsider. What a treasure we have in the Holy Spirit. Thank you Holy Spirit for your comfort and counsel. Fill us afresh this day for all that we may encounter. It's in the name of Jesus we pray, Amen.

Grateful
Thankful
Blessed

Day Twenty Nine

SCRIPTURE:

"In everything give thanks, for this is the will of God in Christ Jesus toward you." - 1 Thessalonians 5:18

PRAYER:

Father, we have much to be grateful for. Breath in our lungs, eyes that see, ears that hear, bodies that move. Most of all, we're grateful for the salvation we've received through your Son Jesus. Our words fall short to describe how thankful we are for this wonderful gift of new life in Christ. May our lives be an expression of our gratitude with each new day of life we're given. It's in Jesus' name we pray, Amen.

Day Thirty

SCRIPTURE:

"Give thanks to the Lord, for he is good; for his loving kindness endures forever." - Psalm 136:1

PRAYER:

Father, we give you thanks for your loving kindness that never ends. The deepest oceans would not be able to contain the grace and mercy You have shown us. We stand in awe of Your kindness that draws us to repentance. When our enemies whisper, 'God isn't good', in our ears, we know that nothing could be further from the Truth. Give us the ability to discern each and every lie that we're offered and to reject it without a second thought. It's in the mighty name of Jesus we pray, Amen.

Day Thirty One

SCRIPTURE:

"Giving thanks always concerning all things in the name of our Lord Jesus Christ, to God, even the Father." - Ephesians 5:20

PRAYER:

Father, we thank you for every detail of our lives. Before we were even conceived, You already had wonderful plans for each of us. We give You thanks for providing our every need and for the endless undeserved gifts we receive on a daily basis. Though none of us is guaranteed tomorrow, we know that nothing can snuff out our lives unless You allow it. You have already ordained our days. Help us to live our lives with gratitude no matter what comes our way. It's in Jesus' name, Amen.

Day Thirty Two

SCRIPTURE:

"In nothing be anxious, but in everything, by prayer and petition with thanksgiving, let your requests be made known to God." - Philippians 4:6

PRAYER:

Father, we confess our tendency to become anxious more often than we would like. We have worried ourselves weary. We have chosen panic over peace. We have been chaotic rather than calm. We have been greedy rather than grateful. So we come before You once again to find rest for our souls and to tap into Your inexhaustible peace that passes all understanding. One by one we lay our cares at Your feet. We choose to be grateful in this moment and give You the praise that you're worthy to receive. Fill us with all the fruits of Your Spirit in order that others might partake of their sweetness. In Jesus' wonderful name we pray, Amen.

God
with
Us

Day Thirty Three

SCRIPTURE:

"Behold, the virgin shall be with child, and shall bring forth a son. They shall call his name Immanuel;" which is, being interpreted, "God with us." - Matthew 1:23

PRAYER:

Jesus, thank you for your willingness to take on flesh and live among us on earth. Your obedience to your Father is the greatest act of humility we can imagine as you briefly stepped out of your place in heaven. You demonstrated what it's like to live in complete union with the Father and Spirit while walking on this planet. Help us to follow in your footsteps in complete obedience to the Father's will. Holy Spirit, empower us to be the hands and feet of Jesus here on earth as long as there's breath in our lungs. In the powerful name of Jesus we pray, Amen.

Day Thirty Four

SCRIPTURE:

"The Lord, your God, is among you, a mighty one who will save. He will rejoice over you with joy. He will calm you in his love. He will rejoice over you with singing." - Zephaniah 3:17

PRAYER:

Father, it fills our hearts with joy to know that You are rejoicing over us with singing. We humbly ask that you implant this singing into every fiber of our being in order that others might be drawn to the song of salvation. May our lives be a melody that echo the songs that are now filling the courts of heaven. We ask that You calm our anxieties with your love. Help us walk according to the beat of your heart in all that we do. In Jesus' mighty name we pray, Amen.

Day Thirty Five

SCRIPTURE:

"Even though I walk through the valley of the shadow of death, I will fear no evil, for you are with me." - Psalm 23:4

PRAYER:

Father, we thank you for being with us no matter what we're going through. We know you're as close to us whether we feel Your presence or not. Not even death can separate us from your love. In Christ we can laugh at evil and the hollow threats it utters. It brings us comfort to know that you walk with us hand in hand as a loving Father scanning the horizon for any possible danger. We place our complete trust in Your promises because we trust the God of those promises. In Jesus' name we pray, Amen.

Day Thirty Six

SCRIPTURE:

"The Lord himself is who goes before you. He will be with you. He will not fail you nor forsake you. Don't be afraid. Don't be discouraged." - Deuteronomy 31:8

PRAYER:

Father, thank you for going before us and fighting on our behalf. How many times have you delivered us from harm even when we didn't realize it? How many times have you blessed our lives without any thanks in return? Though we may be forsaken by others, we have never been forsaken by You. Though we may fail to live out our full potential, we are not failures in Your eyes. Holy Spirit, fill us with boldness to overcome every fear. In the wonderful name of Jesus we pray, Amen.

Day Thirty Seven

SCRIPTURE:

"For where two or three are gathered together in my name, there I am in the middle of them." - Matthew 18:20

PRAYER:

Jesus, thank you for your promise of being right in the midst of our gatherings, even if just two or three. How wonderful to gather with our brothers and sisters who also call upon the name of Jesus for salvation. We can feel Your presence as we come together each week in worship and prayer. We welcome You into our gatherings as we seek your face. Without Your presence, we are nothing but empty clay pots. You are the treasure that gives us value beyond measure! It's in Your name we pray, Amen.

New Beginnings

Day Thirty Eight

SCRIPTURE:

"Therefore if anyone is in Christ, he is a new creation. The old things have passed away. Behold, all things have become new." - 2 Corinthians 5:17

PRAYER:

Father, thank you for making all things new for those in Christ. Only You could have replaced our stony heart with a tender heart. Only You could replace our blind eyes with those that can see. Only You could replace our deaf ears with ears that can now hear your still, small voice. You alone breathe life into dry bones. We wait with anticipation and hope for our future resurrection and the gift of being clothed in a new body. All because of Jesus we pray, Amen.

Day Thirty Nine

SCRIPTURE:

"Therefore we don't faint, but though our outward man is decaying, yet our inward man is renewed day by day." - 2 Corinthians 4:16

PRAYER:

Father, we thank you for the promise that even though we are outwardly wasting away, our spirit is being renewed each new day. Though we are all aging physically, we long to become as little children in our faith. We ask for fresh spiritual strength and energy in order to be victorious over our enemies as long as we have breath in our lungs. As we partake of your Word, nourish our inward man and allow us to share with others we may cross paths with. In Jesus' name we pray, Amen.

Day Forty

SCRIPTURE:

"It is because of the Lord's loving kindnesses that we are not consumed, because his compassion doesn't fail. They are new every morning; great is your faithfulness." - Lamentations 3:22-23

PRAYER:

Father, each new day is a gift from You. In fact, every breath we take is a new and miraculous gift from You. If not for your kindness, we would still be dead in our sins. If not for your new mercy each day, we wouldn't wake up. Thank you for your faithfulness even when we have been unfaithful. Thank you for your forgiveness even when we're less than forgiving toward others. Tenderize our hearts with your great love. Give us an unfailing compassion toward those we encounter on our journey. In the merciful name of Jesus we pray, Amen.

Day Forty One

SCRIPTURE:

"He has made everything beautiful in its time. He has also set eternity in their hearts, yet so that man can't find out the work that God has done from the beginning even to the end." - Ecclesiastes 3:11

PRAYER:

Father, you alone bring beauty from ashes. You alone put broken things back together. In Your hands, we are like broken crayons that still color. Thank you for setting eternity in our hearts. Deep down, every man and woman knows they have been created for something eternal. Yet in our finite human minds, we fail to fully comprehend all that You do behind the scenes. We ask that You transform our lives into a beautiful work of art for your glory. May others see the image of your Son being formed within us. In the glorious name of Jesus we pray, Amen.

Designed
by
God

Day Forty Two

SCRIPTURE:

"For he looked for the city which has the foundations, whose builder and maker is God."
- Hebrews 11:10

PRAYER:

Father, we look to You alone for our future. You are our firm foundation that remains strong no matter what comes our way. Everything You design and build is a masterpiece. Just as Abraham was looking forward to the eternal city You have prepared, we also wait with excitement as citizens of that very city. Until then, we ask that You continue the work that You first began in our lives. We are happy to still be 'under construction' under Your care. It's in Jesus' name we pray, Amen.

Day Forty Three

SCRIPTURE:

"You are the light of the world. A city located on a hill can't be hidden." - Matthew 5:14

PRAYER:

Father, thank you for giving us the Light of Christ that we carry within us everywhere we go. You alone spoke light into our darkness. We ask that others would be attracted to the light we carry. Use us as lanterns to help others find their way to salvation in Christ. We ask for Holy Spirit-led inspiration for creative ways in which we can shine light into darkness. And we ask for the boldness to share the light regardless of the cost. In the mighty name of Jesus we pray, Amen.

Day Forty Four

SCRIPTURE:

"I will give thanks to you, for I am fearfully and wonderfully made." - Psalm 139:14

PRAYER:

Father, we stand in awe when we see Your creative genius. You are the Master Artist in a world of artists. You are the Chief Creator in a world of little creators. When we see the precision and thought You've put into these bodies of ours, we fall to our knees in worship. We see intention in every single cell. Nothing is accidental. From the crown of our head to the soles of our feet, we give You thanks for these walking miracles. We pray this in Jesus' name, Amen.

Day Forty Five

SCRIPTURE:

"God said, 'Let us make man in our image, after our likeness.'"- Genesis 1:26

PRAYER:

Father, even as we lift up this prayer, we are nearing 8 billion people created in Your image! Each one is a unique expression of Your extravagant creativity. We ask that You pour out your Holy Spirit all over the earth in order to draw people from every tribe and nation to Your glorious Son. Open blind eyes and deaf ears so they can see Your goodness and hear the Gospel with understanding. We acknowledge no other gods but You alone. In the beautiful name of Jesus we pray, Amen.

Set

Free

Day Forty Six

SCRIPTURE:

"If therefore the Son makes you free, you will be free indeed." - John 8:36

PRAYER:

Father, thank you for the freedom we have in your Son. In Christ, our freedom is secure in a world of insecurity. Help us to remember this glorious truth when we're tempted to settle for bondage. In the wonderful name of Jesus we pray, Amen.

Day Forty Seven

SCRIPTURE:

"Now the Lord is the Spirit and where the Spirit of the Lord is, there is liberty." - 2 Corinthians 3:17

PRAYER:

Father, thank you for the Holy Spirit that has been poured out upon those of us in Christ. As a result, we can bring freedom wherever we go. Fill us afresh with your Spirit in order to see the atmosphere of our homes, schools, and workplaces change. Most of all, change us from the inside out. In Jesus' name we pray, Amen.

Day Forty Eight

SCRIPTURE:

"Out of my distress, I called on the Lord. The Lord answered me with freedom." - Psalm 118:5

PRAYER:

Father, what a privilege and relief it is to call upon You 24 hours a day. No matter when we call, there's never a busy signal. And, yet, we confess our tendency to call upon you less during the good times. We ask that you deepen our desire to walk more intimately in fellowship with You. We want to be like a little child who spontaneously jumps up into the lap of her papa or mama simply to be close. In the name of our Lord Jesus we pray, Amen.

Day Forty Nine

SCRIPTURE:

"You will know the truth, and the truth will make you free." - John 8:32

PRAYER:

Father, Son, and Spirit, together You are Truth itself. To know you intimately is to walk in true freedom. Thank you Father for willingly giving your Son. Thank you Jesus for willingly purchasing our freedom with the blood you shed on that Roman cross. Thank you Spirit for continually indwelling us and giving us a foretaste of the eternal freedom to come. In the powerful name of Jesus we pray, Amen.

Day Fifty

SCRIPTURE:

"Stand firm therefore in the liberty by which Christ has made us free, and don't be entangled again with a yoke of bondage." – Galatians 5:1

PRAYER:

Lord Jesus, words cannot express our gratitude for the freedom You purchased for us on the cross at Calvary. No longer caged by our sin, we are like birds set free to explore untold horizons from a fresh perspective. When we're tempted to return to our cages of yesterday, remind us of the freedom we've tasted. With the help of your Holy Spirit, we ask for power to continue standing in the true freedom found only in Christ. It's in the soul-freeing name of Jesus we pray, Amen.

Conclusion

It's our hope that the past fifty days have offered some encouragement to you.

Now it's your turn to lift up your heart in prayer as you use God's Word as the launch pad. It really can be as simple as taking one verse of scripture and incorporating it into your own prayer.

In Psalm 1:1-3, we read these words written by David,

"Blessed is the man who doesn't walk in the counsel of the wicked, nor stand on the path of sinners, nor sit in the seat of scoffers; but his delight is in God's law. On his law he *meditates* day and night. He will be like a tree planted by the streams of water, that produces its fruit in its season, whose leaf also does not wither. Whatever he does shall prosper." (emphasis mine)

To "meditate" is to engage in contemplation or reflection; to focus one's thoughts on, reflect on, or ponder over; to think deeply about something; to dwell on any thing in thought; to study; to turn or revolve any subject in the mind; to ruminate."

Did you catch the last word in that definition above? One of the definitions of ruminate is, "to chew repeatedly for an extended period; to chew again what has been chewed slightly and swallowed; chew the cud."

Did you know cows have four stomachs? When a cow begins to eat, it chews the food just enough to swallow it. The unchewed food then travels to the first two stomachs, the rumen (sound familiar?) and the reticulum, where it's stored until later. Eventually, (gross, I know) the cow coughs up bits of the unchewed food called "cud" and chews it completely before swallowing again. The cud then moves on to the third and fourth stomachs.

When we meditate upon God's Word, we are turning it over (chewing it) in our minds before swallowing it and allowing the digestion process of that truth to begin. We find ourselves ruminating on a verse or passage of scripture throughout the day.

When the Word of God goes deep inside of us, we can't help but want to lift up a prayer of response from our hearts. You could say that we're regurgitating our ruminations after partaking of the Book.

As you spend time delighting in the scriptures, may you find yourself praying God's promises and enjoying their many flavors for a lifetime.

CJ and Shelley Hitz

CJ and Shelley Hitz enjoy sharing God's Truth through their speaking engagements and their writing. On downtime, they enjoy spending time outdoors running, hiking and exploring God's beautiful creation.

To find out more about their ministry or to invite them to your next event, check out their website:

www.ShelleyHitz.com

Note from the Author: Reviews are gold to authors! If you have enjoyed this book, would you consider reviewing it on Amazon.com? Thank you!

Download Free Coloring Pages and Printables

- Download over 70 pages of coloring pages, lettering practice sheets, prayer journals, devotionals, and puzzles based on Scriptures from the Navigators Topical Memory System .
- Download these FREE pages and print them as many times as you want for personal use!
- Color, frame, and giveaway. Use them for art for your home or give them away as gifts.

Sign up here:
www.livingcolorsonline.com/free

Happy reading!

Other Books
by CJ and Shelley Hitz

A Heart for Prayer
Encounters with Jesus
Forgiveness Formula
Broken Crayons Still Color
21 Prayers of Generosity
21 Stories of Generosity
21 Days of Generosity Challenge
Unshackled and Free
Fuel for the Soul

And more!

See the entire list here:
www.bodyandsoulpublishing.com/books